a million ways after

A Million Ways After
© 2025 Prior

ALL RIGHTS RESERVED.

No part of this work may be reproduced or transmitted in any form or by any means, electronic or mechanical, including photocopying and recording, or by any information storage or retrieval system without the proper written permission of the appropriate copyright holder listed above, unless such copying is expressly permitted by federal and international copyright law.

ISBN 978-1-964715-08-7

Library of Congress Control Number: 2025908388

Published by Night Song Press. Centreville, Virginia.

First edition.

No artificial intelligence (AI) was used in the generating of this book, and this book may not be used to train AI. All fonts (including the title font, "Democratica") and images are used with commercial license and/or permission.

Cover design by and editing by the author.

Printed in the United States of America.

A million ways after

PRIOR

If you call me a god,
I won't deny it.
I will simply uncreate
The hell it would send me to.

What does this world offer but to be a hero?
Notes left on countertops
Mattresses and "Goddamn clock."
Smiles and food not here to stay

Be a hero or be nothing.

I wish my haters were poets,
And wrote about me.
I'm sure they'd get everything right.
It'd be nice to know myself so well.

The only thing I can say is:
After a breakup
Make sure you're the artist.

The night is dark without you.
Is that normal?

Hatred hides in me
Like a mouse somewhere in this room

It does not come out for traps or cheese
It just hides
Until it suddenly grows so big that furniture falls off its back
Breaking all the domestic peace I trusted
Because they force-fed it

Hatred hides in me.
I won't preach to anyone without admitting it

It hides in me. I didn't always believe in it.

But I believe in it now.

Hatred hides in me.

    Maybe, though,
        A far-fetched hope,

    Maybe it also hides from me.

One thing that comforts me:
No matter how far you went,
In the end of it all

                              My life made a hell of a
                better story.

Almost every year,

I ask the bluebells to wait.
"No," they say, "We are coming now."
I want them to wait until I'm happier
Until things are a little better. I think they'll understand.
"No," they say, "we are coming now."
But it's out of love, I assure them. I just want to be in a
brighter state of mind to admire their beauty. To really
take it in. Just two more weeks would make me ready.
"That's nice," they say, "but we are coming now."
And their green pops up from the cold wet earth
And I sigh at their stubbornness, for they look proud,
like they know what I need better than myself.
So I push the cramps in my neck away and make time
for them amidst the grey clouds in my chest; I think I'll
go sit in the trees as the azure flowers nod at me silently.
I grab my staff at the door. 1
"Our friend?" they say, "Is that you? We thought you
weren't ready."

"No," I say, taking my first step, and looking up. "I am
coming now."

What a paradise we destroyed
To build this paradise.

When that song comes on
And I think about those times you leaned on my chest
And dreamed of the life I'd give you
The land I'd buy
And fall with you through
You're a good hurt.
I hope I'm a good hurt.

Two palm readers
At two different times
Told me my great love would come late in life.
I imagine when we meet at last, I will learn that he was
too busy spinning bottles
Breaking hearts
Kicking up dirt in the sky
When he got mad
To realize he had the patience to love, even see, someone
like me.

I'll look down smiling like a fiend
And say, "That makes a lot of sense.

"So was I."

All I'm saying is
We're all just stories in the end.

You watch his hands touch his belt
Undo the buckle with
Jangling anticipation
He pinches the zipper
Pulls down
And digs with his fingers
You hold your breath
And out
Comes
Grasped in his hand
The words:
"Do whatever the hell you want in life."

For a long time there
I thought I was the good guy.

Words hit, hands shook, and for a longer time there,

I was sure I wasn't.

Now

I don't know, guys

Maybe for a long time coming

I'm starting to think I'm the good guy again.

Leaving you
Makes the world seem cold
I miss the way you hum to me
Soothing my aches
And thawing away the ice
Of my woodsman labors

At night, we sleep in separate rooms.
Being together is just too much.
I'd turn you on, and the heat would be unthinkable
The covers tossed and turned
Neither of us getting rest.

So instead, I share the bed with your replacement:
A different relationship, on the surface.
Her heat is slower, more careful.
It creeps up on me from my toes to my chest
Prowling up my body like a feline
Easing in like the drip of a painkiller.
It's nice, until all at once it isn't.
I awake overwhelmed and imprisoned.

I break away and run back to you in the morning.
You've burned me; I've got the scars.
But I just can't seem to leave you.

I return to my desk each day.
Grab your remote.
Aim it down.

I look forward to your comforting beep.

Pleasure sedates you
Let your most burning
Unsatisfied
Desires rewake you.

I sit at the table
And watch you speak across the room
You hold a drink and laugh
I'm not sure how blood moves through me
When my heart is so many strides away

We're older
You're still the object of my eye
I'm smiling
Because now you speak with
hands crossed in front of you
Listening and nodding more than you once did
But you glance at me

Now
Years later
Your hands are crossed behind you
You sway a bit
But I'm no less enamored
And when you look at me
I see the wild you were
Still are
The wild only I knew.

Just before the bridge
He changed his mind and cut through the grass
That led to the river
He wanted to assert what he'd come to know
That he'd always choose rivers over bridges

Is it enough for you that four people think of you every day
Silent in the car at the red light?
Is that legacy enough for you?
See, the problem is
Everyone who knew you,
They were just kids.
They didn't know how to give you
The legacy you deserved
But I will
I will give you the legacy
Befitting a king
I will
But
First
I guess I need to figure out

How to not be one of those kids anymore

You sick of reading about my dead brother yet?

Me too.

Me too.

Sleep.
You loved sleep.
Anywhere could be your bed.
The couch
The car
The stairs.
Wake!
It was like jabbing a cow with a fork;
You groaned, knowing the future.
Knowing you'd have to stir.
The door needs opening.
My foot needs untangling.
The chips are too high.
Just a second, you know.
And then sleep.
You can sleep.
Anywhere could be your bed.
So why the floor, why the tile?
Why the light on?
That's a funny position.

Sleep.
You loved sleep.
Forever would be okay.
But not to me, I need you.
The door needs opening.
My foot needs untangling.
The chips are too high.
Wake up, wont you?
At least moan so I can hear
I'll close the door harder
And twist my foot deeper
And raise the chips another shelf.
Does that convince you?

What will?
Just give me a groan.

Sleep.
I hate sleep.
I'd rather find the ground.
The door has rusted
My foot's gone numb
The chips have all staled.
Wake, you won't.
Maybe neither will I.
I don't believe in now.
I'll dream through time
And close my eyes.
And try to be like you.

Sleep.
I loved sleep.
Anywhere could be my bed.

The strong one
The faithful
I can handle a script
Your castle
Your angel
I am nothing but sick
So hit me
Too soft
You chose me for this
No targets remain
And nothing to miss
Lay your darkness upon me
It won't be returned
Crush your silence upon me
No lessons are learned
Bloody my face
Give me a fat lip
Twist every bone
I'll sink with your ship
I can take it, you know
I can take it
Take it all
The strong one
The faithful
Just watching you fall
I can take it, you know
Hunt me now
Take my peace
Remove more from the empty
Steal further my sleep
I'm not angry
I can take it
You knew that I could
So hit me

Keep hurting
Remind me it's good
Haunt me
Remember
I'll sink with your ship
Haunt me
Please
Just hand me the script

I look heartless
Wanting the simulation theory to be true
The one where no one and nothing is real
Except for me
Where everything is a mirage
Even the ones I love.

But really
That's the only way I can keep you safe—
If you were never real
Then nothing can hurt you
Not even me.

I give up trying to think of poetic ways to say:
It fucks me up when I see you.

I knew our love had limits
But god
I wanted to toe that line forever.

And in a weird way he was proud of her for breaking his heart
'Cause she never dreamed she'd have that chance
And he never dreamed he'd let her

If I were a ghost
I'd lean against the hull of Titanic
And watch the motes float by in blackness
For days
Everything behind me.

I'd glide above the moons of Jupiter
And gaze
And gaze

I'd go back in time and stand in the tower
Before it fell
To hear the last words and
Be part of it

See, we all have FOMO
Even for the tragedies

Especially for the tragedies

If I were a ghost I'd live
Every life that ever did

I know why you went
Why the white cone drifts
The others judge you. "What is so damn important down
there?" they say
As they hold themselves up on the table
Panting
A cane to the side
And meatloaf passed around in a crackly tin
For the hundredth time
I look up at the trees and think "I know why they went."
But I don't say it
Because it's our secret
And they won't understand
Those who take when they have
And have because they take
The rest would be appalled if they dug inside me and
found
What parts of you are now everywhere
I know why you went
Why the white cone drifts
Why the white cone drifts
Why the white cone drifts

Stand
    In mist
        With mountains watching.

But figure out

        What it is you guard.

I know I'm gonna write about you
One day
But I'm so glad
I don't need to write about you today.

I cry for who I once was.

No, you damned fool:
Not because I regret
The spit I flung
Like graffiti
On the walls of this city

But because I am him
No longer.

He walked like he wore a magnet around his neck and
the earth was metal:
Pitched forward, tripping every third step
His hair a knotted mess
Mumbling.

On my way to the concert,
I wondered what he'd do with a ticket if I gave him one
Then I realized there's probably already
A concert in his head
Maybe a better one

Sing a song of ghosts, they said
Dress the day with night
Sing of all the hidden words
Breathed against the light

Grey trees in a bed of orange
Fallen

Frost upon the window

Magic sleeps below the earth
Eager to be disturbed

Sing a song of ghosts, they said
Dress the day with night
Sing of all the hidden words
Breathed against the light

A hand on a shoulder
Footsteps go ahead

The dead have a say
If the listener is brave enough

Sing a song of ghosts, they said
Dress the day with night
Sing of all the hidden words
Breathed against the light

Dance with fire and shadows thrown
Mulling bitter spices

Cold

Linger

Call the gone
To stay

Spaces complete the circle drawn within the windblown
straw

I sang a song of ghosts today
I dressed the day with night
I sang of all the hidden words
Breathed against the light

2020, a Poem:

Fuck.

I been sitting here a while

On the porch right where it's warm
Past the door, a wide platform
With windows glowing on my arm
I been sitting here a while.

I know each board and how it creaks
I've studied these old nails for weeks
The rails I think are made of teak
I been sitting here a while.

There's food galore inside
A fire for yuletide
And laughter side by side
I been sitting here a while

I guess it might be better in,
Protected from the streets of gin
Foul weather and hearts of tin
I been sitting here a while.

I don't want to be out there, either
I'm not exactly part of that theater
I'm in-between wallpaper and ether
I been sitting here a while

Beyond the dark is cold
Under the roof is safe I'm told
But I think there's also danger in the fold
So I been sitting here a while

It's easy to accept others as they are
When you decide what it is they are
So I want to be close, but also far
I been sitting here a while.

I'll be sitting here a while.

I fear what can hurt me the least
You cannot move
You do not weep
Your face, it stretched
Your lips, they're too thin
Is this why I fear you? The iceberg within?
The dead cannot harm, their hand won't lash out
Their words will not sting
Their eyes will not pout
Our silence is loud
With the summer I freeze
The rest all around seem to tick
Seem a breeze
It's over, it's done
Your cane wobbles no more
The fox can't amuse you
You grumbled; I roar
And like all good lovers, you had to fade
Lie on that pillow
Fall into the shade
Go on your way while I stumble behind
I've left you there
But ahead in my mind
So gently you'll sink and rise gently like yeast
You know what I fear:
What can hurt me the least
Your body, your skin, they're a relic of you
But you, oh my darling, are a relic of me too

Dad's hands on the counter. Eyes down.
"Dad."
Now eyes on eyes.
Dad's mouth open. Words hang themselves from his lips.
A step closer. Bag still packed at the door, just in case. Standing there.
Dad's voice twisted. "You've missed a lot."
His hand on eyes now.
Son's hands on shoulders.
Dad's hands on shoulders
Hands everywhere.

Cool wind.
Lights checkering rectangles.
Against the sky
Dresses. Ties.
Newcomers tumbling in with lanyard passes.
Lean on the rail.
Spotlights across the way.
"There?"
"Afterparty."
Lift lanyard. Read.
Let lanyard fall.

Here's to the mess of us.
The ones below the moral definite
Here's to your filth
Which made mine clean
Shades of identical black that somehow contrast
For just you and me.
To us.
Here's to the mess of us.

Running out of names
To hide the hurt for a while
Too easy to find
They've got my signal on file

Go on. Stand up. Brush it off. Don't complain.
We liked you best when you hid all the pain.

I'm a young man, a new one, I'm learning the ropes.
You've had more time than I did to choose better hopes

Brother and Father, Uncle and god
Hunter and hunted, flawer and flawed

Nice guys finish last
I didn't write that oath
Gladiatorial take first
I tried to be both

It's never enough
I can't be everything they say
I'm not blacker than night
While as scorching as day

I'm not drowning you in ocean at the same time I'm dry
I'm not deep underground and learning to fly

So call it all what you want
I don't negotiate with hate
Take a little and run
Then spit on the gate

Behind shadows it's safe for your ugliness to rest
Tuck it in
Rock it well
Mother knows best

But on sight of my coming
After the rites I'll soon pass
Scatter all that is left of you
Nice guys finish last?

Brother and Father, Uncle and god
Hunter and hunted, flawer and flawed

Commander, Bear, 7593

You should be scared of every name of me.

Whatever the fuck you were behind that screen
I miss you

We want less to be loved
Than to be known.

Caught between fire and water are we
Harden like lava and tether the sea
Like balls on a chain
We're dragged through the grain
What great crumbling mountains we'd be

But I am not nearly like you
You're six-foot-a-million, I'm two
You're fish and I'm crab
You're laughing I'm mad
Out of cerulean and aqua you're blue

So countries load cannons with these
They rumble the grid lines and keys
At our steps the grounds crack
It's a tightrope we lack
And differences again bloody knees

Islands of ourselves do we make
Closing our ports in each wake
I'd be a little white speck
Under the U in Quebec
And you'd be the vowel in lake

Eyes swim in gold
And they bounce like pinballs
To a flash here, a glint there. And oh, I hope,
I imagine so
That long ago
Some greater strike of light blinded them
So that spots and shapes all floated around like dandelion fuzz
And removed their sensitivity to what truly shines
Without metal.

Klimt's Ms. Adele, with her luscious dress falling from her
In folds of glittering wheat, has the glaucoma of glamor, looking dreamily aside.
But the eyes on her, why, maybe they were spared.
Those eyes look not on the riches of what shovels can bring,
On the karats to the left and right.
No, their vision beholds the real light.
You, before the canvas, who stands with the nakedness of your soul alone,
You look at this painting,
A smile on your lips,
A tickle of being watched,
And observe in wonder
As the painting looks back.

You do not understand poems
You are my dog
I love you.

Plump dog, happy
Limping into the room.
Eyes bright, tongue out
Looking always for food.

Heavy breathing getting louder
Nails clack on tile
Finally you see him
Rounding the corner
Head bobbing up and down
Coming to you
Because you're eating lunch

Plump dog, happy
Limping into the room.
Eyes bright, tongue out
Looking always for food

A plate on a tray
First barked at
Then pushed
"No, Max, you're too fat!"
He tilts his head
To slurp it up anyway
Forks fall to the ground

Plump dog, happy
Limping into the room.
Eyes bright, tongue out
Looking always for food

His limping makes him look
Like a pirate ship
Rocking over the swells
As he sails around the house
Eating popcorn covered in dust

Plump dog, happy
Limping into the room.
Eyes bright, tongue out

Looking always for food

Make it home, open arms
Lean down to catch him
He ignores your love
And uses his nose to shove aside your knees
Licking the Panda Express
Stuck on your pants

Plump dog, happy
Limping into the room.
Eyes bright, tongue out
Looking always for food

In the firelight on the dog bed
He snores
Dreaming of chicken
And cookies
Sausage
Anything we will give him
For a hop and a jolly woof

Plump dog, happy
Limping into the room.
Eyes bright, tongue out
Looking always for food

It's all he lives for it seems
He looks at you and smiles
But I let him have any bit he wants
Because he is fourteen
And one day he won't want food anymore
The day my heart will break
So he can have everything

Plump dog, happy
Limping into the room.
Eyes bright, tongue out
Looking always for food

Family means leaving the table in anger
And returning an hour later,
Your plate of food still there
After the dishes were done.

After a while of knowing how to write
I fear
Your words become candy
All taste

I remember it.
That place in the living oak.
Come back there with me.

Can I hide what was meant to be, planting dirt in the sky?
Or can shadow and pitch be held in my hand—Can I greet a goodbye?

Heat on leather, exhaust warbles the air
Were we meant for this speed
Does it encourage us to care?

Gas drips like an IV
My doctor is the steering wheel

                                        Don't mind the brakes

Little Bluebird in the Tree,

Go away.
Not every poem is about you.
Jesus.

The most insulting thing someone ever said to me
Wasn't meant to be hurtful.
She said, "You know, from my view, these shelves were blocking you
All I could see was your head.
So, to me, you glided by
Like an ice skater, smooth, and I had to double-take."
She smiled and I caught my breath
Registering the pain
Because I wanted to step closer and say,
"My darling girl, do you know the way I walk?
Do you not see it?
As I move I feel myself pulsing up and down with the purchase of pavement;
I see myself crossing my hands behind my back as Churchill leaving a room;
My arm lifts and points to the building I am speaking of;
I feel the dirt break as I climb into the next page of woods I meant to reread.
Darling girl, am I the drifting cloud you describe?
Do I not move with the drum beat rhythm of you?
Do you know the way I walk?
Or am I the only one?"

Acknowledgements

Thank you to Samuel, Pat, Wendy, John, and Matt.

Appendix

The poem "Caught between fire and water are we…" is titled "Islands" and its dedication is:

This poem is dedicated to my 6th grade English teacher, Mrs. Anderson. It has absolutely nothing to do with her. One day I arrived to her class and totally forgot it was Poem Day. Freaking Poem Day! All we had to do was pick any poem and read it. ANY DAMN POEM. The boy to my right read SPONGEBOB LYRICS. I had nothing. I, in a tiny, humiliation-ridden voice, only said, "I forgot it was Poem Day" when my name was called. The lip pucker and disappointed, deep eyes of Mrs. Anderson followed by a little "Hmm" haunted my pride for years as I was quickly discarded and attentions moved on to the next student poet. I hung my head in the circle of shame–I mean, desks. I asked not for a make-up assignment or the opportunity to turn it in late. I accepted my fate and vowed then to make it up to dear Mrs. Anderson somehow. Years passed as I plotted my return to grace. I attended her son's wedding, danced and ate, all the while wondering, behind her sparkling earrings and overjoyed smile, "Does she remember Poem Day?" Is she thinking of Poem Day RIGHT NOW as she is clapping for the Best Man's speech? What if HE had forgotten Speech Day? Would there be a disappointed pucker? Does Poem Day haunt her in the shadows of her bed covers too? Does Poem Day stir up questions of what if, or how could it have been? I will receive no grade for this, but finally, at last, it is here. My redemption. My second chance. Mrs. Anderson, not only do I present you with a poem, but it is a poem dedicated to YOU! Yes, YOU! Mrs. Mary Evelyn Anderson. This is your poem given to you with my love and my apologies. May Poem Day be avenged. May justice reign. May my honor be restored on this day.

TL/DR: Mrs. Anderson, this one's for you.

The poem "I fear what can hurt me the least..." is titled "Saints of Alnwick" and its dedicated is:

For Mr. Logan

The poem "Eyes swim in gold..." is titled "Eyes Swim in Gold" and expresses thoughts on the artwork *Portrait of Adele Bloch-Bauer I* by Gustav Klimt. Its dedication is:

For Liz

About the Author

Prior is the pseudonym of an award-winning author of novels, nonfiction, screenplays, and poetry. He's an American in his twenties. When not writing, Prior enjoys cigars, golf, beekeeping, and the woods. He lost his brother to a drug overdose.

Prior chose the shade of anonymity because, while mysterious to the outside, it brought out something not mysterious at all—something well-known and very real—within.

He sends his love to you. Contact his publisher, Night Song Press, to connect.

www.ingramcontent.com/pod-product-compliance
Lightning Source LLC
Chambersburg PA
CBHW020129070526
44107CB00165B/1336/J